MOODS OF
KENT

ANDREAS BYRNE

HALSGROVE

First published in Great Britain in 2007

British Library Cataloguing-in-Publication Data
A CIP record for this title is available from the British Library

ISBN 978 1 84114 617 1

HALSGROVE
Halsgrove House, Ryelands Farm Industrial Estate,
Bagley Green, Wellington, Somerset TA21 9PZ
Tel: 01823 653777 Fax: 01823 216796
email: sales@halsgrove.com
website: www.halsgrove.com

Printed and bound by D'Auria Industrie Grafiche, Italy

I would like to thank the following organizations for allowing me to use the photographs taken on their properties:
Museum of Kent Life (Cobtree Manor Farm)
Leeds Castle, Hever Castle and The National Trust

Introduction

Kent is the second largest county in England and with the highest population. It has three major motorways, one international airport, and one major shipping port, Dover being the busiest in Europe. One Channel Tunnel with a rail network linking Paris to London. Bluewater, the biggest shopping centre in Europe and the Thames Gateway project which plans to build thousands of new houses!

Now, you might think with all this construction, tarmac, shops and houses that there is nothing left for the landscape photographer to take pictures of, but Kent has a great deal to offer in the way of photographic opportunities. The coastline is the longest in the United Kingdom and has been an inspiration to many artists, most famously Turner. The coastline starts in the north of the county with the Thames Estuary, moving along towards the North Sea and around the east coast to meet the Channel. This coastal landscape varies dramatically from marshland and muddy estuaries to shingle and sandy golden beaches ending up with the famous white cliffs at Dover.

Off the beaten track and inland there can be found peaceful villages with charming old inns, village greens and the iconic oast-houses surrounded by orchards, the scenery which inspired H.E.Bates to write *The Darling Buds of May* The North Downs roll all through Kent and are a haven for rare chalkland flowers and an abundance of butterflies and other insects. Kent is home to some of England's most magnificent castles and has more listed buildings and sites of archaeological interest then any other county.

This book is mainly about the beautiful landscapes that can be found in and around Kent. I have also included some flora and fauna as they are also part of the landscape. It's not all blue skies and sunshine although we get a lot of that. A bit of sunshine can transform a scene from the rather bland and uninspiring to the glorious and uplifting. I prefer to take my pictures in the early morning or in the late afternoon as the light takes on a warmer glow with the sun being lower in the sky. This in turn creates longer shadows making for better three dimensional and interesting images. I also like to include water in my landscapes as this adds another element. It can be puddles, ponds, rivers, wet estuary mud or the sea, anything that might give a reflection and gives me two pictures for the price of one!

Getting a reflection in a landscape usually requires sunshine and no wind and is an altogether pleasant experience. This wasn't the case for my picture of a rowing boat on Oare Marshes. There was a bitter north wind blowing through like a freight train and I was being buffeted whilst huddled round my tripod early one January morning. Trying to keep warm whilst waiting for the sun to pop out from behind a cloud I had to get up and run round just to get the blood pumping. At one point I even contemplated driving home and was just about to give up hope when all of a sudden the sun broke through and I was able to concentrate on taking the picture. That's the way of landscapes. Just when you have run out of patience and decide to pack up a moment of inspirational light emerges from nowhere and all the frustration disappears – well, until the next time!

Andreas Byrne

MAP OF KENT

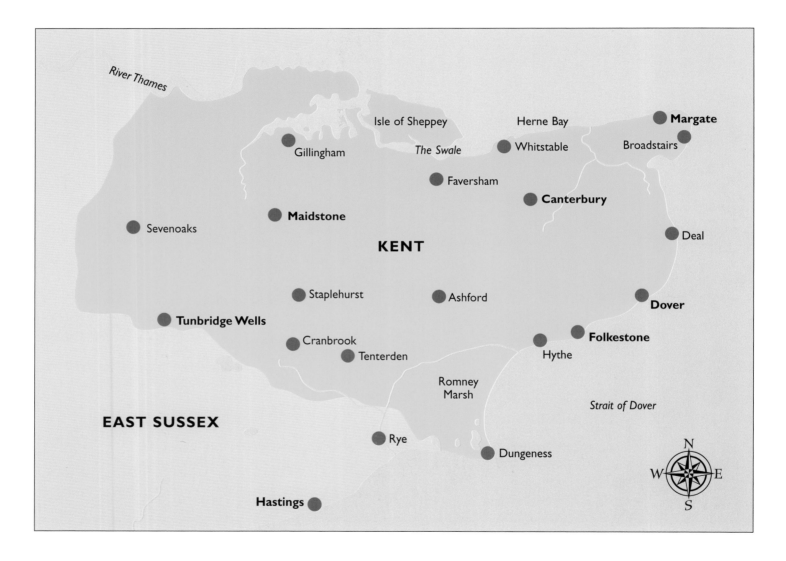

Reflected Oast-house, Yalding
The early morning sunshine lights up these iconic oasts near Yalding, giving a perfect reflection in the River Medway.

Rowing Boat, Oare Marshes
This tranquil scene of a tied up rowing boat and blue skies belies the fact that
there was a freezing north wind blowing over the estuary marshes at Oare.

View over the North Downs, Trottiscliffe
The beautiful morning light streaks across the North Downs overlooking the village of Trottiscliffe.

Rain over Shellness
A distant heavy shower of rain falls from the morning winter skies off the coast at Shellness.

St Clement's Church
An early morning start allowed me to capture this reflection of St Clement's church
at Old Romney on a cool and frosty January morning.

Sunset, Pegwell Bay
A clear winter sunset over the sands of Pegwell Bay, silhouettes the cooling towers of the power station at Sandwich.

Aylesford in Snow
Aylesford is a picturesque village at any time of year, but the overnight snow has transformed the village into a Christmas card image.

QE2 Bridge in the Afternoon
The Queen Elizabeth the Second Bridge spans the River Thames between Dartford
in Kent and Thurrock in Essex, and carries over 150,000 cars and lorries a day.

Reed Reflections, Shorne Country Park
The hues of autumn are upon us as the trees change from greens to reds,
here reflected in one of the fishing ponds at Shorne Country Park.

Horsemonden Church Rapefield
A rain storm had just passed through and the sunlight returned once again
over Horsemonden church, here surrounded by a rapefield.

Cobtree Manor Farm, Winter
A frozen pond and snow on the roof of the oast-houses at Cobtree Manor Farm on a winter's morning.

Bluebells, Crockham Hill
An inviting path through the fragrant bluebells at Crockham Hill woods is a stunning sight in April.

Leeds Castle and Balloons
Hot air balloons reflected in and drifting across the moat at Leeds Castle during the September balloon festival.

Red and White Beach Huts, Tankerton
Colourful beach huts sit along the shoreline at Tankerton.

Sunrise, St Margaret's Bay
A spectacular pink and yellow sunrise at St Margaret's Bay. This is the place
from which to swim the Channel, oh no… I forgot my trunks!

Sunrise over Shellness

This is a naturist beach in summer, but this picture was taken in winter. The sun pierced through the early morning cloud and streaked (pun intended!) over the sea and onto the beach at Shellness.

Broadstairs
An early summer's morning sees the beach at Broadstairs after it has been vacuumed by the litter tractor.
The beach is deserted except for a few gulls by the tide line. By 10am it will be packed.

St Mary's Church, Fawkham, Spring
Late spring comes to this field full of buttercups at St Mary's church near Fawkham.
The next day the mowers returned it to a mown meadow.

Rolvenden Windmill
Spring lambs enjoy an afternoon of sunshine and grass in this rural setting close to Rolvenden Windmill.

Ash Church and Bales
Summer harvesting has arrived with all the dust and scent of dry cut straw hanging in the air.
These rolled bales await the farmer with his tractor and trailer, in a field opposite the church at Ash.

Fly Agaric Toadstools
Autumn has arrived at Beacon Wood Country Park as the fairytale toadstools (fly agaric)
push up from under the ground and form clusters around the silver birch trees.

Sunset over Whitstable
It's a warm still summer's evening as the sun sinks over the horizon,
the two yachts reflected in the calm waters at Whitstable Bay.

Cliff Reflections, St Margaret's Bay
The brilliant white cliffs at St Margaret's Bay are reflected in one of the many pools left
by the receding tide. These cliffs are part of the White Cliffs Country Trail at Dover.

Ash Cricket Pitch in Snow
There'll be no balls bowled today unless they're snowballs! Winter delivers
a blanket of snow to Ash Cricket Club and the surrounding area.

Reculver Towers, Dawn
The sun was just about to rise over the sea on this cool July morning. The coloured
sky has silhouetted Reculver Towers against the glowing promise of a hot day.

Sunset over Swale Marshes
Shellness meets Swale Marshes as the sun goes down. The marshes are tidal and are home to many wading birds.

Sailing Barges, Faversham
When the tidal creek at Faversham is full the reflections of the sailing barges are at their best.
The barges were used to ferry goods up and down the Thames and around the coast of Britain.

Cobtree, Autumn
The morning sun brings out the blue skies and autumn colours around the duck
pond at Cobtree Manor Farm. Cobtree houses the Museum of Kent Life and
demonstrates how oast-houses were used to dry hops for making beer.

Sunrise, Dungeness
The sun rises over the fishing boat sitting on the shingle slopes at Dungeness. In May the
shingle is transformed by the coastal flowers that grow in this moving landscape.

Lady Irene
The morning sun lights up the huge stretch of shingle coastline at Deal, while *Lady Irene* waits to go fishing.

Deal Castle
Deal Castle sits only a few metres from the shingle beach and was used to defend the
coast of Kent in years gone by. Fishing boats with lobster pots await the rising tide.

Fairfield Church Frost
It was a cool crisp winter's morning and the grass was covered with a thick frost at Fairfield
church on Romney Marsh. The frost soon melted and the sheep began to graze.

Fairfield Church Reflection
Fairfield church is surrounded by small waterways which sometimes flood leaving the church stranded.
The low evening light adds a warm glow to the reed bed and its reflection.

Reculver and Tidal Pool
On a summer's evening the sun sets over the sea. The last rays of the sun light
up the tidal pools leading the eye through the picture towards Reculver.

Reculver and Sand Cliffs
The cliffs around Reculver take on a rich warm hue as the sun goes down.
The cliffs are soft and are home to many sand martins.

Trottiscliffe Church, Cornfield
Locally-pronounced Trosley nestles at the bottom of the south slope of the Downs.
A burial chamber, the Coldrum Stones lies nearby, close to the Pilgrims Way.

Boat Reflection, Oare
The mirrored image of two boats anchored in the still waters off Oare Marshes.
Oare Marshes are a haven for wildfowl and a great attraction for bird watchers.

Sheep Drinking out of the Medway
Sheep drinking out of the River Medway on a hot dry afternoon in late summer.
The oast-houses in the background are a common feature of the Kent countryside.

Sarre Windmill
Sarre Windmill was built in 1820 and still produces its own flour and porridge oats.

Botany Bay
The chalk stacks of Botany Bay
are a dramatic feature of this
sandy beach on the Isle of Thanet.
The summer sun goes down
over the sea giving the stacks
a pink glow.

Fishing Boat, Dungeness
A wide angle lens and a low viewpoint have emphasized the fishing boat's bow against the blue sea and sky.

Rochester Castle Fireworks
Every year in July Rochester
Castle holds a musical concert
followed by a spectacular
firework display, seen here
reflected in the waters of
the River Medway.

Oast-house and Wallflowers
Oast-houses are a common feature of the landscape in Kent and make for picture postcard rural scenes. Most have been converted into houses since the decline of hop farming.

Dawn over Romney Marsh
Dawn rises over Romney Marsh on a freezing winter's morning. The Romans reclaimed
Romney Marsh from the sea and used the rich pasture for sheep grazing.

Fence Post, Romney
Fence posts divide the rain sodden meadows of Old Romney on a clear February morning.

Mote Farm Oasts
The four oasts of Mote Farm are situated in a peaceful corner of Kent near Ightham Mote.

Toy's Hill
Backlit beech trees highlight the wonderful autumn colours of Toy's Hill.
Many walks are managed by the National trust.

Frozen Fishing Pond, Shorne
Frozen fishing ponds and frosty reeds are illuminated by the winter sun
on a December morning at Shorne Country Park.

St Margaret's Bay Beach
The beach and white cliffs of St Margaret's Bay glow to a golden yellow as the sun comes out from behind a drifting cloud.

St Mary's Church, Winter
The Norman church of St Mary's at Fawkham sits in a bright winter wonderland.

Trottiscliffe Oast
This is one of many inhabited oast-houses in Kent.
This one in Trottiscliffe makes an attractive and unusual dwelling.

Pegwell Bay
Golden cliffs at Pegwell Bay are reflected in the sand-rippled beach on this December afternoon.
A hover port used to operate from Pegwell Bay but now it's a bird reserve.

Row of Beach Huts
This colourful row of beach huts lines the shingle beach at Tankerton, a quiet seaside resort near Whitstable.

Snowy Lane
A snowy lane follows the tractor tracks into the countryside near Ash.

Ash Church and Snow
Ash church in the grip of winter is surrounded by snow fields. The Norman church
rafters are also home to rare bats which like to join in with the Christmas midnight mass service.

Winter Scene, Ash
A sprinkling of snow lies frozen on the ground as the clouds close in for another dusting over the farmland.

St Mary's, Autumn
Looking like a scene from New England in the Fall, St Mary's church at
Fawkham, with its tiny wooden tower, nestles amongst the autumn trees.

Horsemonden Church and Cornfield
Afternoon light streaks across the golden fields of barley with Horsemonden church in the background.

Ightham Oast in Rape Field
The rape fields add their glorious yellows to the landscape as evening falls over the oast-house near Ightham Mote.

Lullingstone Castle
Lullingstone Castle is the family mansion of the Hart Dykes. It recently featured on
the BBC programme about the castle and the making of the World Garden.

Rochester Castle and Cathedral
Rochester Castle and Cathedral stand majestically above the River Medway. The castle is a fine
example of Norman architecture and the cathedral is the second oldest in the country.

Ightham Mote
The medieval moated manor house is surrounded by beautiful gardens and woodlands.
The National Trust has recently restored this beautiful building.

Woodchurch Windmill
The windmill at Woodchurch, a white smock mill, was built in 1820 and is now fully restored to good order.

The Leather Bottle
Many of Charles Dickens' books refer to people and places in Kent. He was a frequent
visitor to The Leather Bottle public house in the delightful village of Cobham.

Sunset over Minnis Bay
In the summer time the sun sets over the sea on the north Kent coast.
Here at Minnis Bay it transforms the landscape into a palette of pinks and purples.

Sunrise, Broadstairs
Sand ripples and tidal pools are given the Midas touch as the sun rises over the beach at Broadstairs.

Frosty Footpath
Frozen crops and solid earth are gradually warmed by the touch of the morning sun on this footpath near Hartley.

Meopham in the Snow
A wintry scene on the village green at Meopham as snow clouds gather once more.

Sunset near Westgate
As the sun sets and the tide comes in a long finger
of golden light stretches across the sea near Westgate.

Grasses, Shellness
Grasses blow in the cold north wind as early
morning sunlight illuminates the beach
and breakwaters at Shellness.

Crescent Moon over Reculver
The sun had set over the horizon on this warm July night whilst the
crescent moon sat high above the silhouetted towers of Reculver.

Hever Castle
Crocuses abound, spring is just around the corner on this lovely afternoon at Hever Castle.

QE2 Bridge at night
Traffic trails streak as commuters make their way back home through the
Dartford Tunnel or over the Queen Elizabeth the Second Bridge.

The Mausoleum
The old mausoleum in Cobham woods used to belong to the Darnley family and had fallen into disrepair.
The National Trust has now taken it over and it's fully restored.

***Emma Jayne*, Dungeness**
A snow storm was looming over Dungeness as the last rays of sun lit up
one of the fishing boats on the shingle beach on a January afternoon.

Rochester at Night
Lights from Rochester Castle and Cathedral streak over the River Medway early one evening in January.

Chartwell
Chartwell was the family home of Winston Churchill and now belongs
to the National Trust; an old apple tree frames the grand house.

Trees Silhouetted Sunrise
A winter morning dawns, silhouetting the beech trees against a myriad of colours – pinks, purples and oranges.

Beech Trees at Ash
A cold and misty morning in early November. The warm sun breaks through to light the path towards Ash church.

Wood Anemones
Wood anemones carpet the woodland floor in a welcome return to spring and new life in the woods at Shorne.

Two Trees in Corn Field, Ash
The late summer evening light brings out the warmth in this cornfield, with its two trees and summer skies above.

Frosty Boatyard
A freezing morning on Higham Marshes, the morning light bringing an orange glow to the two yachts tied up for the winter.

Fishing Boats, Dungeness
A row of fishing boats at Dungeness, waiting for the tide to turn before sliding down a shingle bank into the sea.

The Lonesome Pine
As the sun sets, the skies take on
the colours of yellow and pink.
Cue Laurel & Hardy, 'Trail of
the Lonesome Pine'

Wreck, Higham Marshes
This abandoned wreck on Higham Marshes sits high and dry on a shingle bank
overlooking the Thames, providing a habitat for tidal sea life.

RX383 Boat and Gulls
A fishing boat returns with its catch to the shores of Dungeness accompanied by a flock of raucous seagulls.

The Ploughed Field
The lines of the ploughed field follow the lines of the footpath along towards Cobham.
This whole area is in the process of being redeveloped and expanded into a new country park.

Autumn Tree, Camer Park
The golden, vibrant colours of autumn are highlighted on this acer tree in Camer Park,
Meopham, which has a wide variety of beautiful mature specimen trees.

Tree Sunburst
Shafts of autumn sunlight burst through the early morning mist creating
a spectacular display at Ashenbank Woods near Cobham.

Kentish Plover
A Kentish plover sits on the sea shore. The Kent shoreline is an important stopping
place for many migrating birds, providing good feeding grounds and nesting places.

Rusting Wreck, Rainham Creek
This rusting wreck on Rainham Creek sits stranded on the mud, unlike my
Wellington boots which sank and are still there to this day!

Matfield Pond Reflection
A lull in the breeze allowed me to capture this brief reflection on the village pond at Matfield one afternoon in March.

Swans at Sunset, Higham Marshes
Walking over Higham Marshes on a late winter's afternoon I came across these
swans who were inquisitive enough to come close to my camera.

Wood Sorrel
Spring is a wonderful time for flowers and I found this wood sorrel growing on a fallen tree near the River Darent in late April.

Sunset over Chillenden Windmill
A southerly wind had blown in high cloud and made the sky very misty, allowing me
to photograph the not so bright sun setting behind Chillenden Windmill.

Cricket, Meopham Green
Summer's arrived! Cricket is played out on the Green at Meopham on the first day of the new season.

Ramsgate Tall Ships
Tall ships by the quayside at Ramsgate Harbour make a colourful spectacle early one September morning.

Sunrise over the Lees, Yalding
A misty sunrise over the Lees near Yalding, giving the landscape a mystical
feel before the sun's rays get to work burning off the mist within a few minutes.

Mallard Duck
A near perfect reflection of a male mallard duck making his way towards my sandwich!

Scotney Castle
Rhododendrons and the romantic ruin of Scotney Castle which is maintained by the National Trust.

Starfish
A starfish washed up on the shore at Folkestone: luckily for him
the tide was coming in so he wouldn't dry up in the sun.

Heaverham
Springtime, cherry blossom and sunshine arrive at Heaverham, best stop for a pub lunch!

Dover Castle
The magnificent castle of Dover stands high above the town and has seen off many potential invaders to our shores.

Path Towards Sutton-at-Hone
The early morning mist of this April day has almost disappeared
from this rural path towards Sutton-at-Hone.

Barges at Gravesend
Dramatic skies over these moored barges on the River Thames near Gravesend, last resting place of Princess Pocohontas. The power station of Tilbury can be seen in the background.

Margate Reflections
Colourful reflections of the sky and beach huts captured in one of the pools left by the receding tide.

Boats at East Farleigh
A clear blue sky on a warm summer's evening over East Farleigh, with
its medieval bridge and pleasure craft on the River Medway.

Faversham Creek
Oyster Bay house, barges, pleasure boats and yachts in the tidal creek
at Faversham, which is also famous for the Shepheard Neame Brewery.

Grey Heron
A grey Heron waits patiently for his next fish supper! Herons can be quite bold around stocked fishing lakes. This one allowed me to get quite close.

Bluebells, Ightham
The evening light illuminates the top of this oak
tree at Ightham. The bluebells underneath the
oak carpet the woodland floor.

River Darent
The morning mist rises as the sun's rays gets to work
over the stream which is the River Darent. Watercress
beds used to be farmed using the water from the river.

Cherry Blossom
A cherry orchard in full foaming white blossom near Southfleet is a wonderful sight.
Kent is renowned for its fruit growing and exports its produce far and wide.

Oasts and Cherry Blossom, Brenchley
A typical rural scene. Cherry blossom frames an oast-house from the church yard in the village of Brenchley.

Eynsford
Early morning sunshine over the ford at Eynsford.
This is a popular spot for families during the summer months.

Nurstead Church
Nurstead church sits on a small hill surrounded by farmland.
A break in the clouds allows the morning sun to bathe the land.

View over Ightham Oasts
Misty evening light in late April warms the land, illuminating the yellow fields of oil seed rape and the oast-houses near Ightham Mote. There is a bench at the edge of the woods so you can sit back and enjoy the view.

Southfleet Cherry Blossom
The church at Southfleet basking in the morning spring sunshine and framed by some cherry blossom.

Folkestone Harbour
Folkestone Harbour used to be one of the main ports from which to catch the hovercraft
over to France. The Channel Tunnel has made a big difference to passenger travel.

Ferry leaving Dover
Dover is the main place for passenger ferries today and is the busiest port in Europe.
A Norfolk Line ferry leaves Dover bound for foreign lands across the Channel.

Ramsgate Sunrise
A sea mist began to lift over Ramsgate Harbour allowing the watery sunshine to light up the yachts moored in rows. Ramsgate is one of the ferry ports to France.

Broadstairs Harbour
Broadstairs has a tiny harbour, seen here with a few sea-faring vessels.
The sun shimmers off the wet sand left by the outgoing tide.

Margate Sunrise
Margate has a pleasure beach with lovely golden sand and amusements on the seafront.
The beach was empty at this time in the morning as the sun tried to punch its way through the clouds.

South Foreland Lighthouse
The lighthouse at South Foreland sits high on the white cliffs close to Dover and gives spectacular views to France across one of the busiest seaways in the world.

Viaduct, South Darenth
The viaduct at South Darenth carries trains over the river towards London.

Bridge over the Medway, the Lees
The River Medway flows under the fifteenth-century stone bridge near Yalding as the mists of the morning burn off.

Chillenden Windmill
The open trestle post windmill is now fully restored after collapsing in 2003.
It dates from 1868 and is captured here in mellow evening light.

Terry's Butchers, Brenchley
Brenchley has many fine Tudor buildings. Dappled shade casts shadows from an old oak tree over Terry's butcher's shop.

Footbridge over Darent
The River Darent winds its way through the countryside underneath the footbridge that leads to Sutton-at-Hone.

Frosty Gate, Cliffe Pools
A cold bright frosty morning on the marshes at Cliffe Pools.
The RSPB manage the bird reserve which is home to many visiting waders.

Sunset over Pegwell Bay
The tide goes out a long way at Pegwell Bay leaving large tidal pools in its wake.
Walking out to this vast stretch of sand, I photographed the sun setting
over the horizon, turning the landscape shades of pink.

Sunburst over the Sea
A classic picture of 'God's fingers' as shafts of sunlight pierce gaps in the cloud over the sea off the coast of Deal.

Frosty Reeds
A hard overnight frost has transformed the reed beds at Cliffe Pools to a magical scene.

Row of Trees
The warm evening glow on the trees and fields near Southfleet, a favourite with dog walkers.

Boats at Folkestone Harbour
Colourful boats at the old harbour at Folkestone gently move with the outgoing tide.

Autumn Bridge
The first signs of autumn around a footbridge leading across a small stream into the field beyond towards Chiddingstone.

Frosty Fence, Cliffe Pools
Frosty sunshine adds a warm glow to the sometimes bleak marshes at Cliffe Pools.

Low Sunlight, River Darent
Reflections in a quiet corner of the
River Darent near Horton Kirby.

Bluebells
In April Kentish woodlands are transformed into a fragrant sea of blue by the bluebells.
Seen here in a wood on Wrotham Hill.

View over Heaverham
Walkers can enjoy panoramic views whilst walking along the Pilgrims Way, such as this sight towards Heaverham.

Stodmarsh
Night draws in over the River Stour
which runs through Stodmarsh bird
reserve, home to many wild birds.

Luddesdown
This tiny hamlet of Luddesdown is surrounded by a beautiful landscape and woodland
and is bypassed by the Weald Way. The church dates from the thirteenth century.

QE2 Bridge
The Queen Elizabeth the second Bridge spans the River Thames, here photographed from the viewing platform along the public footpath by the side of the river.

ONE MAN WALKING

PHOTOGRAPHS & DESIGN BY MARK CURRIE

In support of The Jordan Legacy and mental wellbeing
(10% of the sale of this book will be donated to the charity)

The Jordan Legacy

I REALLY LIKE WALKING. ALONG COASTAL PATHS. UP HILLS. INTO WOODS. ACROSS MOORS. WALKING IS WHERE I ESCAPE. WALKING IS WHERE I AM AT PEACE WITH MYSELF. WHERE MY HEAD IS HAPPY AND MY MIND IS FREE. I CAN THINK CLEARLY WHEN I'M WALKING, ALTHOUGH SOMETIMES I DON'T THINK MUCH AT ALL. SOMETIMES A GOOD IDEA POPS INTO MY HEAD AND THAT IS EXCITING. SOMETIMES I TAKE A PHOTOGRAPH. I ALWAYS *FEEL MORE* AND SEE MORE WHEN I AM WALKING. SOMETIMES I LISTEN TO MUSIC, ALTHOUGH MOST OF THE TIME I LIKE THE SOUND OF NOTHINGNESS. JUST THE WIND AND THE BIRDS. I LOVE THE SOUND OF THE SEA AND RAIN, OR SNOW FALLING AND THE ROLL OF THUNDER. I LIKE WALKING WITH OTHERS AND TALKING TO THE ODD STRANGER. BUT I AM HAPPY BEING ALONE. OPEN SPACES WITH NO ONE AROUND ARE BEST. NOT QUITE KNOWING WHERE I AM OR WHERE I'M GOING IS EVEN BETTER. ADMIRING THE VIEW. TAKING AN OCCASIONAL BREAK. DRINKING MY COFFEE. LYING ON MY BACK LOOKING UP AT THE SKY. WANDERING AROUND FOR HOUR AFTER HOUR. UNDER HOT SUN OR DARK CLOUD. I LOVE IT ALL. LAUGHING AT MY MISHAPS OR OCCASIONAL WRONG TURNS. AND AS I EAT UP THE MILES, I SEE THE END IN SIGHT. MY LEGS STRONG BUT NICELY TIRED. AND FEELING THE INNER SATISFACTION OF REACHING MY GOAL.

MARK CURRIE

Taking Flight, Otley 2018

Sniffing the Trail, Malham 2018

Circling the Castle, Holy Island 2022

Snowed Under, Otley 2016

Five Penguins, Redcar 2018

Big Head, near Barnoldswick 2022

Sea Fishing, Berwick-Upon-Tweed 2022

Iron Man, Crosby 2018

Old Couple, Redcar 2018

White House, Otley 2018

Chevin Gate, Otley 2018

Two Horses, Llwyndafydd 2019

Three Sheep, Worston 2021

Smoke Signal, East Morton, 2019

Old Shooting Hut, Denton Moor 2020

Angry Sky, Formby 2018

Big Mouth, Out Newton 2018

Wooden Puffin, Bempton Cliffs 2018

Bird Watchers, Bempton Cliffs 2018

Gargoyles, Timble 2021

Space Invader, Timble 2021

Abandoned Car, Otley 2020

Fortune Teller, Otley 2022

Seagull, New Quay 2019

Dead Seal, Ravenscar 2021

Snapping the Harbour, Lanzarote 2019

The Chosen One, Lanzarote 2019

Defunct Steelworks, Redcar 2018

Pier Towers, Withernsea 2018

Fluffy Clouds, Farnley 2018

Tyre Swing, Farnley 2018

Wheelies, Birmingham 2019

Rolling Surf, Saltburn 2018

Big Rock, Matlock 2021

Storm Coming, Matlock 2021

Space Walkers, Mount Teide, Tenerife 2017

Lava Rock, Mount Teide, Tenerife 2017

Snow Storm, Malham 2019

Misty Moor, Thimbleby 2018

Tiptoeing by Tulips, Pocklington 2019

Walking in Circles, Barden 2021

Top Withins, Haworth 2021

Pushing up Daisies, Appletreewick 2017

White Car, Otley 2021

River Revellers, Otley 2022

Puffin Wall, John O'Groats, 2020

The Doorway, Castle Douglas 2018

Lobster Pots, Saltburn 2021

Corrugated Shed, Port Mulgrave 2021

Freezing, Otley Nature Reserve 2016

Snow Tunnel, The Chevin, Otley 2022

Stone Shelter, Denton Moor 2018

Outside No.9, Denton Moor 2021

People Pointing, Morston 2018

Windmill, Burnham Overy Staithe 2018

Gull Goes Fishing, Bempton 2022

In Between Cliffs, Flamborough 2022

Stone Knuckles, near Ingelborough 2022

Waiting for a Train, Ribblehead 2018

He's Following Me, West Lulworth 2019

Durdle Door, Lulworth Cove 2019

The Estuary, Blakeney 2018

Beachgoers, West Runton 2018

The Canal, Crossflatts 2017

Human Hamster, Galloway Forest Park 2018

Hanging Around, Pendle Hill 2022

Sunken Village, Thruscross 2022

Thatched Barn, Grimwith Reservoir 2022

Rolling Hills, Worston 2019

View from Snowden, Wales 2016

The Tower, Blacko 2018

Transfixed, Aysgarth Falls 2020

Hill Top Puddles, Beamsley 2021

White Hut, Koh Madsum, Thailand 2017

Orange House, Ban Tern, Thailand 2017

Sea Looker, Cha-am, Thailand 2020

Pond Paradise, Cha-am, Thailand 2020

Churn Clough Reservoir, Sabden 2020

Looking South, New Quay 2019

Lighthouse, Hunstanton 2018

By the Bench, Sheringham 2018

Winter Sky, Newall with Clifton 2020

Passenger Ferry, Lake District 2012

Dead Slow, Bridlington 2018

Pleasure Beach, Blackpool 2019

On the Rocks, Staple Island 2022

High Platform Low Tide, Holy Island 2022

Bird on Wire, Jersey 2011

One Man Walking, Kilnsea 2018

Acknowledgement

I would like to dedicate this book to all those people whose lives have been affected by suicide and adverse mental health.
That's why I am very happy to support The Jordan Legacy and their quest for positive mental wellbeing.

Mark Currie, One Man Walking

Every day in the UK, 17 people die by suicide. More men and women under 35 lose their lives this way than by cancers, diabetes, heart attacks or road traffic accidents. Each suicide will directly or indirectly impact 135 other people, from the first responder, to a loved one, friend, colleague and others who knew that person. There is a cost to the UK economy of £1.7 million for every suicide, with the majority of that money being used to support those bereaved. There is hope, though: if we all learn to look after our physical and mental wellbeing better, if we can better understand the impact poor mental health has and how to spot the signs in ourselves and others and if we all just take a moment to ask our friend, 'How are you really?' then we will begin to move toward a zero suicide society.

Steve Phillip, founder of The Jordan Legacy CIC

First published in 2022 by Catapult Books

© 2022 Catapult Books.
All photographs © Mark Currie

Written and designed by Mark Currie

www.catapultfilms.co.uk/books

ISBN: 978-0-9568581-4-6

A CIP Catalogue of this book is available from
the British Library

Printed in UK by:
Print Crew Ltd